YOUR JOURNAL OF OVERCOMING

GRIEF

This journal is to help track your moods, energy level, mental health and more, to find your triggers and spot any spirals into unhealthy thought patterns and work through depression, guilt, loneliness and other symptoms of grief. This journal can help you keep track of diet, exercise, medications, self-care, therapy, overall mood and more. Use it to write down your thoughts and feelings and to supplement your therapy with worksheets and mindfulness exercises.

With weekly stress and mood journals, symptom and self-care checklists and small worksheets.

This journal also has gratitude prompts and inspirational quotes to encourage self-care and a positive mindset. To help refocus your mind on your bad days and remind you why life is GREAT!

This book is also a journal with many lined pages in this journal your thoughts and track achievements on the lined pages.

DAILY ENERGY vs MOOD TRACKER

TRACK YOUR DAILY ENERGY AND MOOD USING DIFFERENT COLOURS ON THIS LINE CHART - NOTE YOUR TRIGGERS BELOW.

100

75

50

25

0

ENERGY

| MONDAY | TUESDAY | WEDNESDAY | THURSDAY | FRIDAY | SATURDAY | SUNDAY | MO |

GRIEF MENTAL HEALTH SYMPTOM TRACKER

	FREQ. / SEVERITY Y/N	MON	TUES	WED	THURS	FRI	SAT	SUN
USED COPING SKILLS AND EFFECTIVENESS	Y/N 0-5							
FEELING SAD OR HOPELESS	0-5							
DIFFICULTY CONCENTRATING	0-5							
FEELING RESTLESS	0-5							
FEELING IRRITABLE	0-5							
DIFFICULTY SLEEPING	0-5							
FEELINGS OF GUILT	0-5							
OVER SLEEPING	Y/N							
FEELING LONELY	0-5							
PARTICIPATED IN SOCIAL ACTIVITIES	Y/N							
APPETITE (0-1 BEING UNDEREATING, 4- 5 BEING OVEREATING)	0-5							
ENERGY LEVELS	0-5							
ENJOYED HOBBIES OR ACTIVITIES	Y-N							
RELATIONSHIP PROBLEMS	0-5							
CRIED AT SOME POINT DURING THE DAY	Y/N							
SUICIDAL THOUGHTS	0-5							
FEELINGS OF NUMBNESS OR APATHY	0-5							
MOOD SWINGS	0-5							
STOMACH PROBLEMS OR NAUSEA	Y/N							
FEELING ANXIOUS / WORRYING / FEARFUL	0-5							
FEELINGS OF LONGING	0-5							
SELF ESTEEM	0-5							
SELF-CARE ACTIVITIES	Y/N							
FEEL OVERWHELMED	Y/N							
ATTENDED THERAPY	Y/N							
LOGGED DIARY	Y/N							

CONTINUE TO THE NEXT PAGE

GRIEF MENTAL HEALTH SYMPTOM TRACKER

	FREQ. / SEVERITY Y/N	MON	TUES	WED	THURS	FRI	SAT	SUN
EXERCISE	MINS							
FEELING CALM	0-5							
FEELING HAPPY	0-5							
FEELING PRODUCTIVE	0-5							
WORK/SCHOOL STRESS	0-5							
GENERAL STRESS	0-5							
SPOKE TO SOMEONE ABOUT FEELINGS	Y/N							
FELT GRIEF TODAY	Y/N 0-5							
FEELINGS OF IMPROVEMENT	Y/N 0-5							
DEPRESSION	Y/N 0-5							
MEDICATION:	DOSE							
MEDICATION:	DOSE							
MEDICATION:	DOSE							

FILL IN THE CHARTS TO TRACK SYMPTOMS AND THEN PUT DETAILS AND POST POSSIBLE TRIGGERS IN THE NOTES BELOW.

_____
_____
_____
_____
_____
_____
_____
_____
_____
_____
_____
_____
_____

HOW OFTEN DID YOU FILL OUT THIS CHART

NOT AT ALL   [ ]   1-3X PER WEEK   [ ]   ALMOST EVERY DAY   [ ]   EVERYDAY [ ]

WHAT I DID TODAY

MONDAY
_____

TUESDAY
_____

WEDNESDAY
_____

THURSDAY
_____

FRIDAY
_____

SATURDAY
_____

SUNDAY
_____

TODAY I FELT...

MONDAY
_____

TUESDAY
_____

WEDNESDAY
_____

THURSDAY
_____

FRIDAY
_____

SATURDAY
_____

SUNDAY
_____

WHAT DOES GRATITUDE MEAN?

ANSWER THESE QUESTIONS TO BREAK OUT OF NEGATIVE THOUGHT PATTERNS AND REFOCUS ON THE THINGS THAT MAKE YOU HAPPY AND GRATEFUL.

_____

_____

_____

_____

_____

_____

_____

_____

_____

_____

_____

_____

_____

_____

_____

_____

_____

_____

_____

_____

_____

_____

_____

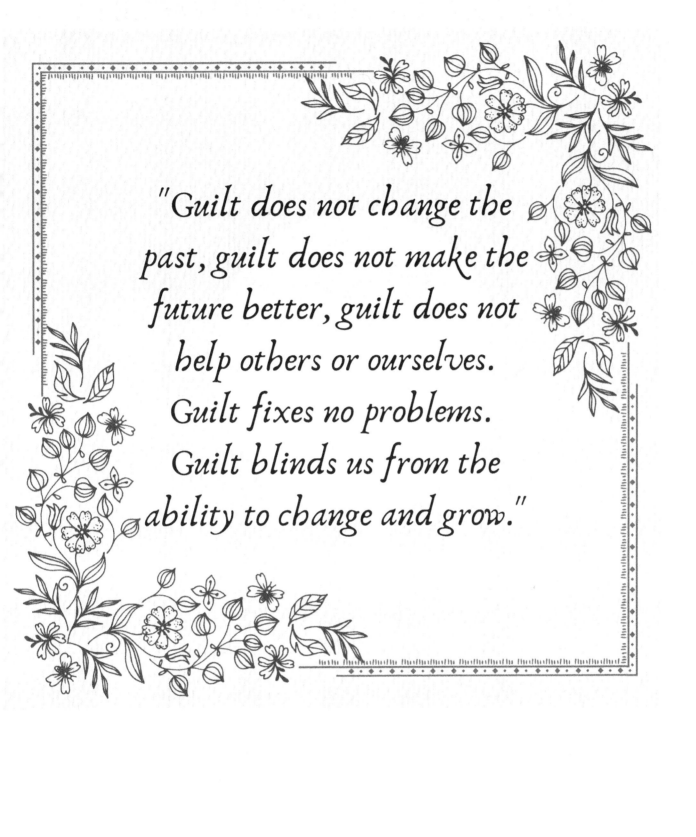

"Guilt does not change the past, guilt does not make the future better, guilt does not help others or ourselves. Guilt fixes no problems. Guilt blinds us from the ability to change and grow."

DAILY ENERGY vs MOOD TRACKER

TRACK YOUR DAILY ENERGY AND MOOD USING DIFFERENT COLOURS ON THIS LINE CHART - NOTE YOUR TRIGGERS BELOW.

100

75

50

25

0

| MONDAY | TUESDAY | WEDNESDAY | THURSDAY | FRIDAY | SATURDAY | SUNDAY |

ENERGY

MO

GRIEF MENTAL HEALTH SYMPTOM TRACKER

	FREQ. / SEVERITY Y/N	MON	TUES	WED	THURS	FRI	SAT	SUN
USED COPING SKILLS AND EFFECTIVENESS	Y/N 0-5	☐	☐	☐	☐	☐	☐	☐
FEELING SAD OR HOPELESS	0-5							
DIFFICULTY CONCENTRATING	0-5							
FEELING RESTLESS	0-5							
FEELING IRRITABLE	0-5							
DIFFICULTY SLEEPING	0-5							
FEELINGS OF GUILT	0-5							
OVER SLEEPING	Y/N							
FEELING LONELY	0-5							
PARTICIPATED IN SOCIAL ACTIVITIES	Y/N							
APPETITE (0-1 BEING UNDEREATING, 4- 5 BEING OVEREATING)	0-5							
ENERGY LEVELS	0-5							
ENJOYED HOBBIES OR ACTIVITIES	Y-N							
RELATIONSHIP PROBLEMS	0-5							
CRIED AT SOME POINT DURING THE DAY	Y/N							
SUICIDAL THOUGHTS	0-5							
FEELINGS OF NUMBNESS OR APATHY	0-5							
MOOD SWINGS	0-5							
STOMACH PROBLEMS OR NAUSEA	Y/N							
FEELING ANXIOUS / WORRYING / FEARFUL	0-5							
FEELINGS OF LONGING	0-5							
SELF ESTEEM	0-5							
SELF-CARE ACTIVITIES	Y/N							
FEEL OVERWHELMED	Y/N							
ATTENDED THERAPY	Y/N							
LOGGED DIARY	Y/N							

CONTINUE TO THE NEXT PAGE

GRIEF MENTAL HEALTH SYMPTOM TRACKER

	FREQ. / SEVERITY Y/N	MON	TUES	WED	THURS	FRI	SAT	SUN
EXERCISE	MINS							
FEELING CALM	0-5							
FEELING HAPPY	0-5							
FEELING PRODUCTIVE	0-5							
WORK/SCHOOL STRESS	0-5							
GENERAL STRESS	0-5							
SPOKE TO SOMEONE ABOUT FEELINGS	Y/N							
FELT GRIEF TODAY	Y/N 0-5	☐	☐	☐	☐	☐	☐	☐
FEELINGS OF IMPROVEMENT	Y/N 0-5	☐	☐	☐	☐	☐	☐	☐
DEPRESSION	Y/N 0-5	☐	☐	☐	☐	☐		☐
MEDICATION:	DOSE							
MEDICATION:	DOSE							
MEDICATION:	DOSE							

FILL IN THE CHARTS TO TRACK SYMPTOMS AND THEN PUT DETAILS AND POST POSSIBLE TRIGGERS IN THE NOTES BELOW.

_____
_____
_____
_____
_____
_____
_____
_____
_____
_____
_____
_____

HOW OFTEN DID YOU FILL OUT THIS CHART

NOT AT ALL   [ ]   1-3X PER WEEK   [ ]   ALMOST EVERY DAY   [ ]   EVERYDAY   [ ]

WHAT I DID TODAY

MONDAY
_____

TUESDAY
_____

WEDNESDAY
_____

THURSDAY
_____

FRIDAY
_____

SATURDAY
_____

SUNDAY
_____

TODAY I FELT...

MONDAY
_____

TUESDAY
_____

WEDNESDAY
_____

THURSDAY
_____

FRIDAY
_____

SATURDAY
_____

SUNDAY
_____

WHEN IS GRATITUDE IMPORTANT?

ANSWER THESE QUESTIONS TO BREAK OUT OF NEGATIVE
THOUGHT PATTERNS AND REFOCUS ON THE THINGS THAT MAKE
YOU HAPPY AND GRATEFUL.

The loss is immeasurable but so is the love left behind

DAILY ENERGY vs MOOD TRACKER

TRACK YOUR DAILY ENERGY AND MOOD USING DIFFERENT COLOURS ON THIS LINE CHART - NOTE YOUR TRIGGERS BELOW.

100

75

50

25

0

ENERGY

| MONDAY | TUESDAY | WEDNESDAY | THURSDAY | FRIDAY | SATURDAY | SUNDAY |

GRIEF MENTAL HEALTH SYMPTOM TRACKER

	FREQ. / SEVERITY Y/N	MON	TUES	WED	THURS	FRI	SAT	SUN
USED COPING SKILLS AND EFFECTIVENESS	Y/N 0-5							
FEELING SAD OR HOPELESS	0-5							
DIFFICULTY CONCENTRATING	0-5							
FEELING RESTLESS	0-5							
FEELING IRRITABLE	0-5							
DIFFICULTY SLEEPING	0-5							
FEELINGS OF GUILT	0-5							
OVER SLEEPING	Y/N							
FEELING LONELY	0-5							
PARTICIPATED IN SOCIAL ACTIVITIES	Y/N							
APPETITE (0-1 BEING UNDEREATING, 4- 5 BEING OVEREATING)	0-5							
ENERGY LEVELS	0-5							
ENJOYED HOBBIES OR ACTIVITIES	Y-N							
RELATIONSHIP PROBLEMS	0-5							
CRIED AT SOME POINT DURING THE DAY	Y/N							
SUICIDAL THOUGHTS	0-5							
FEELINGS OF NUMBNESS OR APATHY	0-5							
MOOD SWINGS	0-5							
STOMACH PROBLEMS OR NAUSEA	Y/N							
FEELING ANXIOUS / WORRYING / FEARFUL	0-5							
FEELINGS OF LONGING	0-5							
SELF ESTEEM	0-5							
SELF-CARE ACTIVITIES	Y/N							
FEEL OVERWHELMED	Y/N							
ATTENDED THERAPY	Y/N							
LOGGED DIARY	Y/N							

CONTINUE TO THE NEXT PAGE

GRIEF MENTAL HEALTH SYMPTOM TRACKER

	FREQ. / SEVERITY Y/N	MON	TUES	WED	THURS	FRI	SAT	SUN
EXERCISE	MINS							
FEELING CALM	0-5							
FEELING HAPPY	0-5							
FEELING PRODUCTIVE	0-5							
WORK/SCHOOL STRESS	0-5							
GENERAL STRESS	0-5							
SPOKE TO SOMEONE ABOUT FEELINGS	Y/N							
FELT GRIEF TODAY	Y/N 0-5	☐	☐	☐	☐	☐	☐	☐
FEELINGS OF IMPROVEMENT	Y/N 0-5	☐	☐	☐	☐	☐	☐	☐
DEPRESSION	Y/N 0-5	☐	☐	☐	☐	☐	☐	☐
MEDICATION:	DOSE							
MEDICATION:	DOSE							
MEDICATION:	DOSE							

FILL IN THE CHARTS TO TRACK SYMPTOMS AND THEN PUT DETAILS AND POST POSSIBLE TRIGGERS IN THE NOTES BELOW.

_____
_____
_____
_____
_____
_____
_____
_____
_____
_____
_____
_____

HOW OFTEN DID YOU FILL OUT THIS CHART
NOT AT ALL   [ ]   1-3X PER WEEK   [ ]   ALMOST EVERY DAY   [ ]   EVERYDAY   [ ]

WHAT I DID TODAY

MONDAY
_____
_____

TUESDAY
_____
_____

WEDNESDAY
_____
_____

THURSDAY
_____
_____

FRIDAY
_____
_____

SATURDAY
_____
_____

SUNDAY
_____
_____

TODAY I FELT...

MONDAY
_____
_____

TUESDAY
_____
_____

WEDNESDAY
_____
_____

THURSDAY
_____
_____

FRIDAY
_____
_____

SATURDAY
_____
_____

SUNDAY
_____
_____

WHO ARE YOU MOST GRATEFUL FOR?

ANSWER THESE QUESTIONS TO BREAK OUT OF NEGATIVE THOUGHT PATTERNS AND REFOCUS ON THE THINGS THAT MAKE YOU HAPPY AND GRATEFUL.

It's okay to ask for help.

DAILY ENERGY vs MOOD TRACKER

TRACK YOUR DAILY ENERGY AND MOOD USING DIFFERENT COLOURS ON THIS LINE CHART - NOTE YOUR TRIGGERS BELOW.

100							
75							
50							
25							
0	MONDAY	TUESDAY	WEDNESDAY	THURSDAY	FRIDAY	SATURDAY	SUNDAY

ENERGY

GRIEF MENTAL HEALTH SYMPTOM TRACKER

	FREQ. / SEVERITY Y/N	MON	TUES	WED	THURS	FRI	SAT	SUN
USED COPING SKILLS AND EFFECTIVENESS	Y/N 0-5							
FEELING SAD OR HOPELESS	0-5							
DIFFICULTY CONCENTRATING	0-5							
FEELING RESTLESS	0-5							
FEELING IRRITABLE	0-5							
DIFFICULTY SLEEPING	0-5							
FEELINGS OF GUILT	0-5							
OVER SLEEPING	Y/N							
FEELING LONELY	0-5							
PARTICIPATED IN SOCIAL ACTIVITIES	Y/N							
APPETITE (0-1 BEING UNDEREATING, 4- 5 BEING OVEREATING)	0-5							
ENERGY LEVELS	0-5							
ENJOYED HOBBIES OR ACTIVITIES	Y-N							
RELATIONSHIP PROBLEMS	0-5							
CRIED AT SOME POINT DURING THE DAY	Y/N							
SUICIDAL THOUGHTS	0-5							
FEELINGS OF NUMBNESS OR APATHY	0-5							
MOOD SWINGS	0-5							
STOMACH PROBLEMS OR NAUSEA	Y/N							
FEELING ANXIOUS / WORRYING / FEARFUL	0-5							
FEELINGS OF LONGING	0-5							
SELF ESTEEM	0-5							
SELF-CARE ACTIVITIES	Y/N							
FEEL OVERWHELMED	Y/N							
ATTENDED THERAPY	Y/N							
LOGGED DIARY	Y/N							

CONTINUE TO THE NEXT PAGE

GRIEF MENTAL HEALTH SYMPTOM TRACKER

	FREQ. / SEVERITY Y/N	MON	TUES	WED	THURS	FRI	SAT	SUN
EXERCISE	MINS							
FEELING CALM	0-5							
FEELING HAPPY	0-5							
FEELING PRODUCTIVE	0-5							
WORK/SCHOOL STRESS	0-5							
GENERAL STRESS	0-5							
SPOKE TO SOMEONE ABOUT FEELINGS	Y/N							
FELT GRIEF TODAY	Y/N 0-5	☐	☐	☐	☐	☐	☐	☐
FEELINGS OF IMPROVEMENT	Y/N 0-5	☐	☐	☐	☐	☐	☐	☐
DEPRESSION	Y/N 0-5	☐	☐	☐	☐	☐	☐	☐
MEDICATION:	DOSE							
MEDICATION:	DOSE							
MEDICATION:	DOSE							

FILL IN THE CHARTS TO TRACK SYMPTOMS AND THEN PUT DETAILS AND POST POSSIBLE TRIGGERS IN THE NOTES BELOW.

_____
_____
_____
_____
_____
_____
_____
_____
_____
_____
_____
_____
_____

HOW OFTEN DID YOU FILL OUT THIS CHART

NOT AT ALL   [ ]   1-3X PER WEEK   [ ]   ALMOST EVERY DAY   [ ]   EVERYDAY   [ ]

WHAT I DID TODAY

MONDAY
_____
_____

TUESDAY
_____
_____

WEDNESDAY
_____
_____

THURSDAY
_____
_____

FRIDAY
_____
_____

SATURDAY
_____
_____

SUNDAY
_____
_____

TODAY I FELT...

MONDAY
_____
_____

TUESDAY
_____
_____

WEDNESDAY
_____
_____

THURSDAY
_____
_____

FRIDAY
_____
_____

SATURDAY
_____
_____

SUNDAY
_____
_____

"Grief never ends...but it changes. It's a passage. Not a place to stay."

WHAT I HOPE IS YET TO COME...

ANSWER THESE QUESTIONS TO BREAK OUT OF NEGATIVE THOUGHT PATTERNS AND REFOCUS ON THE THINGS THAT MAKE YOU HAPPY AND GRATEFUL.

DAILY ENERGY vs MOOD TRACKER

TRACK YOUR DAILY ENERGY AND MOOD USING DIFFERENT COLOURS ON THIS LINE CHART - NOTE YOUR TRIGGERS BELOW.

100

75

50

25

0

ENERGY

MONDAY	TUESDAY	WEDNESDAY	THURSDAY	FRIDAY	SATURDAY	SUNDAY

MOO

GRIEF MENTAL HEALTH SYMPTOM TRACKER

	FREQ. / SEVERITY Y/N	MON	TUES	WED	THURS	FRI	SAT	SUN
USED COPING SKILLS AND EFFECTIVENESS	Y/N 0-5							
FEELING SAD OR HOPELESS	0-5							
DIFFICULTY CONCENTRATING	0-5							
FEELING RESTLESS	0-5							
FEELING IRRITABLE	0-5							
DIFFICULTY SLEEPING	0-5							
FEELINGS OF GUILT	0-5							
OVER SLEEPING	Y/N							
FEELING LONELY	0-5							
PARTICIPATED IN SOCIAL ACTIVITIES	Y/N							
APPETITE (0-1 BEING UNDEREATING, 4- 5 BEING OVEREATING)	0-5							
ENERGY LEVELS	0-5							
ENJOYED HOBBIES OR ACTIVITIES	Y-N							
RELATIONSHIP PROBLEMS	0-5							
CRIED AT SOME POINT DURING THE DAY	Y/N							
SUICIDAL THOUGHTS	0-5							
FEELINGS OF NUMBNESS OR APATHY	0-5							
MOOD SWINGS	0-5							
STOMACH PROBLEMS OR NAUSEA	Y/N							
FEELING ANXIOUS / WORRYING / FEARFUL	0-5							
FEELINGS OF LONGING	0-5							
SELF ESTEEM	0-5							
SELF-CARE ACTIVITIES	Y/N							
FEEL OVERWHELMED	Y/N							
ATTENDED THERAPY	Y/N							
LOGGED DIARY	Y/N							

CONTINUE TO THE NEXT PAGE

GRIEF MENTAL HEALTH SYMPTOM TRACKER

	FREQ. / SEVERITY Y/N	MON	TUES	WED	THURS	FRI	SAT	SUN
EXERCISE	MINS							
FEELING CALM	0-5							
FEELING HAPPY	0-5							
FEELING PRODUCTIVE	0-5							
WORK/SCHOOL STRESS	0-5							
GENERAL STRESS	0-5							
SPOKE TO SOMEONE ABOUT FEELINGS	Y/N							
FELT GRIEF TODAY	Y/N 0-5	☐	☐	☐	☐	☐	☐	☐
FEELINGS OF IMPROVEMENT	Y/N 0-5	☐	☐	☐	☐	☐	☐	☐
DEPRESSION	Y/N 0-5	☐	☐	☐	☐	☐	☐	☐
MEDICATION:	DOSE							
MEDICATION:	DOSE							
MEDICATION:	DOSE							

FILL IN THE CHARTS TO TRACK SYMPTOMS AND THEN PUT DETAILS AND POST POSSIBLE TRIGGERS IN THE NOTES BELOW.

_____

_____

_____

_____

_____

_____

_____

_____

_____

_____

_____

_____

_____

HOW OFTEN DID YOU FILL OUT THIS CHART

NOT AT ALL   [ ]   1-3X PER WEEK   [ ]   ALMOST EVERY DAY   [ ]   EVERYDAY   [ ]

WHAT I DID TODAY

MONDAY
_____
_____

TUESDAY
_____
_____

WEDNESDAY
_____
_____

THURSDAY
_____
_____

FRIDAY
_____
_____

SATURDAY
_____
_____

SUNDAY
_____
_____

TODAY I FELT...

MONDAY
_____
_____

TUESDAY
_____
_____

WEDNESDAY
_____
_____

THURSDAY
_____
_____

FRIDAY
_____
_____

SATURDAY
_____
_____

SUNDAY
_____
_____

"do not allow grief to control your life, instead use it to become a better person"

WHAT DO YOU LOVE ABOUT YOUR FAVOURITE BOOK?

ANSWER THESE QUESTIONS TO BREAK OUT OF NEGATIVE THOUGHT PATTERNS AND REFOCUS ON THE THINGS THAT MAKE YOU HAPPY AND GRATEFUL.

DAILY ENERGY vs MOOD TRACKER

TRACK YOUR DAILY ENERGY AND MOOD USING DIFFERENT COLOURS ON THIS LINE CHART - NOTE YOUR TRIGGERS BELOW.

100

75

50

25

0

ENERGY

| MONDAY | TUESDAY | WEDNESDAY | THURSDAY | FRIDAY | SATURDAY | SUNDAY |

MOOD

GRIEF MENTAL HEALTH SYMPTOM TRACKER

	FREQ. / SEVERITY Y/N	MON	TUES	WED	THURS	FRI	SAT	SUN
USED COPING SKILLS AND EFFECTIVENESS	Y/N 0-5							
FEELING SAD OR HOPELESS	0-5							
DIFFICULTY CONCENTRATING	0-5							
FEELING RESTLESS	0-5							
FEELING IRRITABLE	0-5							
DIFFICULTY SLEEPING	0-5							
FEELINGS OF GUILT	0-5							
OVER SLEEPING	Y/N							
FEELING LONELY	0-5							
PARTICIPATED IN SOCIAL ACTIVITIES	Y/N							
APPETITE (0-1 BEING UNDEREATING, 4- 5 BEING OVEREATING)	0-5							
ENERGY LEVELS	0-5							
ENJOYED HOBBIES OR ACTIVITIES	Y-N							
RELATIONSHIP PROBLEMS	0-5							
CRIED AT SOME POINT DURING THE DAY	Y/N							
SUICIDAL THOUGHTS	0-5							
FEELINGS OF NUMBNESS OR APATHY	0-5							
MOOD SWINGS	0-5							
STOMACH PROBLEMS OR NAUSEA	Y/N							
FEELING ANXIOUS / WORRYING / FEARFUL	0-5							
FEELINGS OF LONGING	0-5							
SELF ESTEEM	0-5							
SELF-CARE ACTIVITIES	Y/N							
FEEL OVERWHELMED	Y/N							
ATTENDED THERAPY	Y/N							
LOGGED DIARY	Y/N							

CONTINUE TO THE NEXT PAGE

GRIEF MENTAL HEALTH SYMPTOM TRACKER

	FREQ. / SEVERITY Y/N	MON	TUES	WED	THURS	FRI	SAT	SUN
EXERCISE	MINS							
FEELING CALM	0-5							
FEELING HAPPY	0-5							
FEELING PRODUCTIVE	0-5							
WORK/SCHOOL STRESS	0-5							
GENERAL STRESS	0-5							
SPOKE TO SOMEONE ABOUT FEELINGS	Y/N							
FELT GRIEF TODAY	Y/N 0-5	☐	☐	☐	☐	☐	☐	☐
FEELINGS OF IMPROVEMENT	Y/N 0-5	☐	☐	☐	☐	☐	☐	☐
DEPRESSION	Y/N 0-5	☐	☐	☐	☐	☐	☐	☐
MEDICATION:	DOSE							
MEDICATION:	DOSE							
MEDICATION:	DOSE							

FILL IN THE CHARTS TO TRACK SYMPTOMS AND THEN PUT DETAILS AND POST POSSIBLE TRIGGERS IN THE NOTES BELOW.

_____
_____
_____
_____
_____
_____
_____
_____
_____
_____
_____
_____
_____
_____

HOW OFTEN DID YOU FILL OUT THIS CHART
NOT AT ALL   [ ]   1-3X PER WEEK   [ ]   ALMOST EVERY DAY   [ ]   EVERYDAY   [ ]

WHAT I DID TODAY

MONDAY
_____
_____

TUESDAY
_____
_____

WEDNESDAY
_____
_____

THURSDAY
_____
_____

FRIDAY
_____
_____

SATURDAY
_____
_____

SUNDAY
_____
_____

TODAY I FELT...

MONDAY
_____
_____

TUESDAY
_____
_____

WEDNESDAY
_____
_____

THURSDAY
_____
_____

FRIDAY
_____
_____

SATURDAY
_____
_____

SUNDAY
_____
_____

Make Your Head A Nice Place To Live.

WHAT MOMENT ARE YOU MOST GRATEFUL FOR?

ANSWER THESE QUESTIONS TO BREAK OUT OF NEGATIVE THOUGHT PATTERNS AND REFOCUS ON THE THINGS THAT MAKE YOU HAPPY AND GRATEFUL.

DAILY ENERGY vs MOOD TRACKER

TRACK YOUR DAILY ENERGY AND MOOD USING DIFFERENT COLOURS ON THIS LINE CHART - NOTE YOUR TRIGGERS BELOW.

100

75

50

25

0

ENERGY | MONDAY | TUESDAY | WEDNESDAY | THURSDAY | FRIDAY | SATURDAY | SUNDAY | MOOD

GRIEF MENTAL HEALTH SYMPTOM TRACKER

	FREQ. / SEVERITY Y/N	MON	TUES	WED	THURS	FRI	SAT	SUN
USED COPING SKILLS AND EFFECTIVENESS	Y/N 0-5							
FEELING SAD OR HOPELESS	0-5							
DIFFICULTY CONCENTRATING	0-5							
FEELING RESTLESS	0-5							
FEELING IRRITABLE	0-5							
DIFFICULTY SLEEPING	0-5							
FEELINGS OF GUILT	0-5							
OVER SLEEPING	Y/N							
FEELING LONELY	0-5							
PARTICIPATED IN SOCIAL ACTIVITIES	Y/N							
APPETITE (0-1 BEING UNDEREATING, 4- 5 BEING OVEREATING)	0-5							
ENERGY LEVELS	0-5							
ENJOYED HOBBIES OR ACTIVITIES	Y-N							
RELATIONSHIP PROBLEMS	0-5							
CRIED AT SOME POINT DURING THE DAY	Y/N							
SUICIDAL THOUGHTS	0-5							
FEELINGS OF NUMBNESS OR APATHY	0-5							
MOOD SWINGS	0-5							
STOMACH PROBLEMS OR NAUSEA	Y/N							
FEELING ANXIOUS / WORRYING / FEARFUL	0-5							
FEELINGS OF LONGING	0-5							
SELF ESTEEM	0-5							
SELF-CARE ACTIVITIES	Y/N							
FEEL OVERWHELMED	Y/N							
ATTENDED THERAPY	Y/N							
LOGGED DIARY	Y/N							

CONTINUE TO THE NEXT PAGE

GRIEF MENTAL HEALTH SYMPTOM TRACKER

	FREQ. / SEVERITY Y/N	MON	TUES	WED	THURS	FRI	SAT	SUN
EXERCISE	MINS							
FEELING CALM	0-5							
FEELING HAPPY	0-5							
FEELING PRODUCTIVE	0-5							
WORK/SCHOOL STRESS	0-5							
GENERAL STRESS	0-5							
SPOKE TO SOMEONE ABOUT FEELINGS	Y/N							
FELT GRIEF TODAY	Y/N 0-5	☐	☐	☐	☐	☐	☐	☐
FEELINGS OF IMPROVEMENT	Y/N 0-5	☐	☐	☐	☐	☐	☐	☐
DEPRESSION	Y/N 0-5	☐	☐	☐	☐	☐	☐	☐
MEDICATION:	DOSE							
MEDICATION:	DOSE							
MEDICATION:	DOSE							

FILL IN THE CHARTS TO TRACK SYMPTOMS AND THEN PUT DETAILS AND POST POSSIBLE TRIGGERS IN THE NOTES BELOW.

_____
_____
_____
_____
_____
_____
_____
_____
_____
_____
_____
_____
_____
_____

HOW OFTEN DID YOU FILL OUT THIS CHART

NOT AT ALL [ ]   1-3X PER WEEK [ ]   ALMOST EVERY DAY [ ]   EVERYDAY [ ]

WHAT I DID TODAY

MONDAY

_____

_____

TUESDAY

_____

_____

WEDNESDAY

_____

_____

THURSDAY

_____

_____

FRIDAY

_____

_____

SATURDAY

_____

_____

SUNDAY

_____

_____

TODAY I FELT...

MONDAY

_____

_____

TUESDAY

_____

_____

WEDNESDAY

_____

_____

THURSDAY

_____

_____

FRIDAY

_____

_____

SATURDAY

_____

_____

SUNDAY

_____

_____

One Minute Meditation

Breathe in through your nose.

Breathe out through your mouth.

Feel air in the depths of your lungs
as you breathe in again.

As you breathe out feel tension
release from your body.

Repeat 3x.

WHAT HAVE YOU SEEN TODAY YOU ARE THANKFUL FOR?

ANSWER THESE QUESTIONS TO BREAK OUT OF NEGATIVE THOUGHT PATTERNS AND REFOCUS ON THE THINGS THAT MAKE YOU HAPPY AND GRATEFUL.

DAILY ENERGY vs MOOD TRACKER

TRACK YOUR DAILY ENERGY AND MOOD USING DIFFERENT COLOURS ON THIS LINE CHART - NOTE YOUR TRIGGERS BELOW.

100

75

50

25

0   MONDAY   TUESDAY   WEDNESDAY   THURSDAY   FRIDAY   SATURDAY   SUNDAY

ENERGY   MOO

GRIEF MENTAL HEALTH SYMPTOM TRACKER

	FREQ. / SEVERITY Y/N	MON	TUES	WED	THURS	FRI	SAT	SUN
USED COPING SKILLS AND EFFECTIVENESS	Y/N 0-5							
FEELING SAD OR HOPELESS	0-5							
DIFFICULTY CONCENTRATING	0-5							
FEELING RESTLESS	0-5							
FEELING IRRITABLE	0-5							
DIFFICULTY SLEEPING	0-5							
FEELINGS OF GUILT	0-5							
OVER SLEEPING	Y/N							
FEELING LONELY	0-5							
PARTICIPATED IN SOCIAL ACTIVITIES	Y/N							
APPETITE (0-1 BEING UNDEREATING, 4- 5 BEING OVEREATING)	0-5							
ENERGY LEVELS	0-5							
ENJOYED HOBBIES OR ACTIVITIES	Y-N							
RELATIONSHIP PROBLEMS	0-5							
CRIED AT SOME POINT DURING THE DAY	Y/N							
SUICIDAL THOUGHTS	0-5							
FEELINGS OF NUMBNESS OR APATHY	0-5							
MOOD SWINGS	0-5							
STOMACH PROBLEMS OR NAUSEA	Y/N							
FEELING ANXIOUS / WORRYING / FEARFUL	0-5							
FEELINGS OF LONGING	0-5							
SELF ESTEEM	0-5							
SELF-CARE ACTIVITIES	Y/N							
FEEL OVERWHELMED	Y/N							
ATTENDED THERAPY	Y/N							
LOGGED DIARY	Y/N							

CONTINUE TO THE NEXT PAGE

WHAT I DID TODAY

MONDAY
_____

_____

TUESDAY
_____

_____

WEDNESDAY
_____

_____

THURSDAY
_____

_____

FRIDAY
_____

_____

SATURDAY
_____

_____

SUNDAY
_____

_____

TODAY I FELT...

MONDAY
_____

_____

TUESDAY
_____

_____

WEDNESDAY
_____

_____

THURSDAY
_____

_____

FRIDAY
_____

_____

SATURDAY
_____

_____

SUNDAY
_____

_____

GRIEF MENTAL HEALTH SYMPTOM TRACKER

	FREQ. / SEVERITY Y/N	MON	TUES	WED	THURS	FRI	SAT	SUN
EXERCISE	MINS							
FEELING CALM	0-5							
FEELING HAPPY	0-5							
FEELING PRODUCTIVE	0-5							
WORK/SCHOOL STRESS	0-5							
GENERAL STRESS	0-5							
SPOKE TO SOMEONE ABOUT FEELINGS	Y/N							
FELT GRIEF TODAY	Y/N 0-5	☐	☐	☐	☐	☐	☐	☐
FEELINGS OF IMPROVEMENT	Y/N 0-5	☐	☐	☐	☐	☐	☐	☐
DEPRESSION	Y/N 0-5	☐	☐	☐	☐	☐	☐	☐
MEDICATION:	DOSE							
MEDICATION:	DOSE							
MEDICATION:	DOSE							

FILL IN THE CHARTS TO TRACK SYMPTOMS AND THEN PUT DETAILS AND POST POSSIBLE TRIGGERS IN THE NOTES BELOW.

_____
_____
_____
_____
_____
_____
_____
_____
_____
_____
_____
_____
_____
_____

HOW OFTEN DID YOU FILL OUT THIS CHART
NOT AT ALL   [ ]   1-3X PER WEEK   [ ]   ALMOST EVERY DAY   [ ]   EVERYDAY   [ ]

DAILY ENERGY vs MOOD TRACKER

TRACK YOUR DAILY ENERGY AND MOOD USING DIFFERENT COLOURS ON THIS LINE CHART - NOTE YOUR TRIGGERS BELOW.

100

75

50

25

0

ERGY

| MONDAY | TUESDAY | WEDNESDAY | THURSDAY | FRIDAY | SATURDAY | SUNDAY |

MOOD

GRIEF MENTAL HEALTH SYMPTOM TRACKER

	FREQ. / SEVERITY Y/N	MON	TUES	WED	THURS	FRI	SAT	SUN
USED COPING SKILLS AND EFFECTIVENESS	Y/N 0-5	☐	☐	☐	☐	☐	☐	☐
FEELING SAD OR HOPELESS	0-5							
DIFFICULTY CONCENTRATING	0-5							
FEELING RESTLESS	0-5							
FEELING IRRITABLE	0-5							
DIFFICULTY SLEEPING	0-5							
FEELINGS OF GUILT	0-5							
OVER SLEEPING	Y/N							
FEELING LONELY	0-5							
PARTICIPATED IN SOCIAL ACTIVITIES	Y/N							
APPETITE (0-1 BEING UNDEREATING, 4- 5 BEING OVEREATING)	0-5							
ENERGY LEVELS	0-5							
ENJOYED HOBBIES OR ACTIVITIES	Y-N							
RELATIONSHIP PROBLEMS	0-5							
CRIED AT SOME POINT DURING THE DAY	Y/N							
SUICIDAL THOUGHTS	0-5							
FEELINGS OF NUMBNESS OR APATHY	0-5							
MOOD SWINGS	0-5							
STOMACH PROBLEMS OR NAUSEA	Y/N							
FEELING ANXIOUS / WORRYING / FEARFUL	0-5							
FEELINGS OF LONGING	0-5							
SELF ESTEEM	0-5							
SELF-CARE ACTIVITIES	Y/N							
FEEL OVERWHELMED	Y/N							
ATTENDED THERAPY	Y/N							
LOGGED DIARY	Y/N							

CONTINUE TO THE NEXT PAGE

GRIEF MENTAL HEALTH SYMPTOM TRACKER

	FREQ. / SEVERITY Y/N	MON	TUES	WED	THURS	FRI	SAT	SUN
EXERCISE	MINS							
FEELING CALM	0-5							
FEELING HAPPY	0-5							
FEELING PRODUCTIVE	0-5							
WORK/SCHOOL STRESS	0-5							
GENERAL STRESS	0-5							
SPOKE TO SOMEONE ABOUT FEELINGS	Y/N							
FELT GRIEF TODAY	Y/N 0-5	☐	☐	☐	☐	☐	☐	☐
FEELINGS OF IMPROVEMENT	Y/N 0-5	☐	☐	☐	☐	☐	☐	☐
DEPRESSION	Y/N 0-5	☐	☐	☐	☐	☐	☐	☐
MEDICATION:	DOSE							
MEDICATION:	DOSE							
MEDICATION:	DOSE							

FILL IN THE CHARTS TO TRACK SYMPTOMS AND THEN PUT DETAILS AND POST POSSIBLE TRIGGERS IN THE NOTES BELOW.

_____
_____
_____
_____
_____
_____
_____
_____
_____
_____
_____
_____
_____
_____

HOW OFTEN DID YOU FILL OUT THIS CHART

NOT AT ALL   [ ]   1-3X PER WEEK   [ ]   ALMOST EVERY DAY   [ ]   EVERYDAY   [ ]

WHAT I DID TODAY

MONDAY
_____

TUESDAY
_____

WEDNESDAY
_____

THURSDAY
_____

FRIDAY
_____

SATURDAY
_____

SUNDAY
_____

TODAY I FELT...

MONDAY
_____

TUESDAY
_____

WEDNESDAY
_____

THURSDAY
_____

FRIDAY
_____

SATURDAY
_____

SUNDAY
_____

WHAT IS THE MOST DELICIOUS FOOD?

ANSWER THESE QUESTIONS TO BREAK OUT OF NEGATIVE THOUGHT PATTERNS AND REFOCUS ON THE THINGS THAT MAKE YOU HAPPY AND GRATEFUL.

"be the things you loved most
about the people who are gone"

Made in the USA
Monee, IL
24 June 2021